LOVE
IS WALKING
HAND IN HAND
BY
CHARLES M.
SCHULZ

ISBN-13:978-1-60433-302-2
ISBN-10: 1-60433-302-2

This book may be ordered by mail from the publisher.
Please include $4.99 for postage and handling.
But please support your local bookseller first!

Books published by Cider Mill Press Book Publishers are available at special discounts
for bulk purchases in the United States by corporations, institutions, and other
organizations. For more information, please contact the publisher.

Cider Mill Press Book Publishers
"Where good books are ready for press"
12 Port Farm Road
Kennebunkport, Maine 04046

Visit us on the web!
www.cidermillpress.com

Design by:
Jason Zamajtuk, Tilly Grassa, Melissa Gerber

Printed in China

1 2 3 4 5 6 7 8 9 10

A PEANUTS CLASSIC Edition

LOVE
IS WALKING
HAND IN HAND

Love is
mussing up
someone's
hair

Love is
loaning your
best comic
magazines

Love
is
having
a
special song

Love

is

tickling

Love is
a valentine
with lace
all around
the edges

Love is
wishing you had
nerve enough to
go over and
talk with that little girl
with the red hair

Love is
letting him win
even though you
know you could
slaughter him

Love is
sharing
your
popcorn

Love is
hating
to say
good-bye

Love is
walking
hand-
in-hand

Love is
a letter
on pink
stationery

Love is
getting someone
a glass of water
in the middle
of the night

Love is passing notes back and forth in school

Love is
standing in
a doorway just
to see her
if she comes
walking by

Love is
making
fudge
together

Love is
wondering
what he's doing
right now this
very moment

Love is
buying
somebody
a present
with your
own money

Love is not nagging

Love is
visiting
a sick
friend

Love is a phone call

Love is
walking
in the rain
together

Love is
eating out
with your
whole family

Love is
being able to spot
her clear across
the playground
among
four hundred
other kids

Love is
committing
yourself
in writing

Love is
meeting
someone
by the pencil
sharpener

Love is
being happy
just knowing
that she's
happy...but
that isn't so easy

Love

is a

flag

Love is

liking

people

Love is liking ideas

Love is
the
whole
world

Other Books by Charles M. Schulz

About Cider Mill Press Book Publishers

Good ideas ripen with time. From seed to harvest, Cider Mill Press strives to bring fine reading, information, and entertainment together between the covers of its creatively crafted books. Our Cider Mill bears fruit twice a year, publishing a new crop of titles each Spring and Fall.

Visit us on the web at
www.cidermillpress.com
or write to us at
12 Port Farm Road
Kennebunkport, Maine 04046

Where Good Books
are Ready for Press

THE
HOUSE
OF
CAINE